The Making of the United Kingdom

WAYLAND

The Making of the United Kingdom 1500-1750

Church and People
Crown and Parliament
Social Change
Unification

Cover: Bishop Sherburne asking Henry VIII to confirm a document, 1547: (inset) Protestants being burnt at the stake in Canterbury in 1555.

Series and Book Editor: Rosemary Ashley
Designer: Joyce Chester

First published in 1996 by Wayland Publishers Ltd, 61 Western Road, Hove, East Sussex, BN3 1JD, England

British Library Cataloguing in Publication Data
Gibb, Christopher, 1955–
   Church and people. – (The making of the
   United Kingdom, 1500–1750)
   1.Religion and state – Great Britain – History –
   Juvenile literature 2.Great Britain – History –
   Modern period, 1485– – Juvenile literature
   I.Title
   941'.05

   ISBN 0 7502 1813 4

Typeset by Joyce Chester
Printed and bound in Italy by G. Canale
C.S.p.A., Turin

Picture acknowledgements
The pictures in this book were supplied by AKG London /Chichester Cathedral cover (main picture), /Vatican Museum 7, /Thyssen-Bornemisza Collection 15, 22; Bridgeman Art Library /British Library 6, /Germanisches National Museum, Nuremburg 10, /Christies 13 (top), /British Library 14, /Private Collection 20, 24, /Victoria and Albert Museum 29, /British Library 30 (lower), /Prado, Madrid 31, /Corsham Court, Wilts 33, /Château de Versailles, France 37, /Private Collection 40; Robert Harding/P. Craven 17; Mary Evans Picture Library cover, 9, 16 (lower), 26, 38, 42; Image Select 12, 28, 32; Wayland Picture Library /British Museum 4, 5, 8, 11, 13 (lower), /National Portrait Gallery 16 (top), 18, 19, 21, 23, /National Portrait Gallery 25, 27, 30 (top), 34, 35, 36, 39, 41, 43 (both), 44.

Contents

1 Catholic Britain
page 4

2 The Reformation
page 10

3 The King's Reformation
page 15

4 Counter Reformation & Compromise
page 20

5 John Calvin and Puritanism
page 26

6 Calvinism in Scotland
page 29

7 The Road to Civil War
page 31

8 Civil War
page 37

9 Moderation and the Age of Reason
page 41

Time Line *page 45*

Glossary *page 46*

Books to Read *page 47*

Places of Interest to Visit *page 47*

Index *page 48*

1

Catholic Britain

In 1500, the people of Britain, like most other Europeans, followed the religion of the Catholic Church. Yet less than 250 years later the majority of Britons were Protestants, belonging to one group or another, while some had ceased to believe in God altogether.

This painting shows an attractive scene of peasants at work in the years leading up to 1500. In fact their lives were spent in hard, brutal labour.

In medieval life, the priest's role was all-important. This fifteenth-century print shows a priest giving the last rites to a dying woman. His assistant carries a lantern and a bell to announce to the community that another soul is on its way to heaven.

This change did not take place peacefully. Indeed, the sixteenth and seventeenth centuries were years of extreme religious intolerance. Today we think of religion as a personal matter between an individual and his or her God. How then do we explain a period in history when people would torture, burn and massacre one another because they held different religious beliefs – even though they all claimed to worship the same Christian God?

We can only begin to understand if we try to see life through the eyes of families living through these times. For most people life was very hard. Towns and cities were tiny (the city of London in 1500 had a population of 50,000 – about the size of a medium-sized country town today). Most people lived in villages, supporting themselves from produce grown on small pieces of land. Disease and famine swept the country regularly, and more than half the children born would die in infancy.

No wonder then that religion, with its promise of a better life in the next world (after death), was so important to the people of medieval Britain. The life of the village centred around the parish church, with its Latin services (which ordinary people could not understand), its Saint's Days, images and holy relics.

A manuscript painting illustrating a priest saying a mass for the dead in church. Saying masses for the souls of dead people was considered essential if they were to reach heaven.

The priest played a vital role, for it was only he who could administer the rites of the Catholic Church – such as baptism, marriage and the forgiveness of sins. He was believed by many of his congregation to have almost magical powers. At the centre of Catholic worship was the mass, during which the priest held up bread and wine which were believed to be transformed into the body and blood of Jesus Christ.

Monasteries and convents played an important part in the medieval Catholic Church. In these buildings monks and nuns retreated from the world to dedicate themselves to a life of prayer and meditation. Many people went on pilgrimages to monasteries, some of which contained shrines believed to hold the bodies or relics (remains) of saints. Miracles of healing were often reported to take place at such shrines. The monasteries also acted as an important 'safety net' for the poor, providing shelter, care for the sick and alms.

The leader of this vast Christian organization was the Pope, who was believed to be God's representative on Earth. From the Vatican Palace in Rome he ruled over cardinals, bishops and abbots, right down to the humblest parish priest. The Pope also claimed supreme power over kings and emperors, which entitled him to settle quarrels between them – although this power was far from being accepted by many rulers.

The Pope, the head of the Catholic Church, lived in Rome, often in great luxury. This painting, by Bartolomeo Sacchi, shows Pope Sixtus IV (1414–85) surrounded by attendants.

The Church provided a sense of unity for society in a dangerous world. Everyone had a place, whether that person was a pope, monarch, lord or peasant. To break this unity, it was thought, would result in chaos. Both Catholics, and later Protestants, believed this – a belief that resulted in the brutality used by both sides when dealing with their enemies if they seemed to threaten the stability of society.

However, by 1500, cracks were appearing in the rigid grip which the Church held on the medieval world. The rediscovery of Greek and Roman literature by a group of scholars headed by the philosopher Erasmus, led them to question some of the Church's claims. Linked to this was a growth in education, largely resulting from the recent invention of the printing press. Previously, books had been laboriously copied by hand and read mainly by churchmen. Now hundreds of copies could be produced in a few days and distributed throughout Europe. This gave people the opportunity to read and study the work of scholars.

The discovery of the Americas and the riches of India and the Far East also broadened people's outlook and resulted in a growth in trade. This brought about the arrival of a new class of bankers and merchants, who often resented the power of the Church and its abuses, such as its control over money-lending and trade.

Desiderius Erasmus [c.1466–1536]

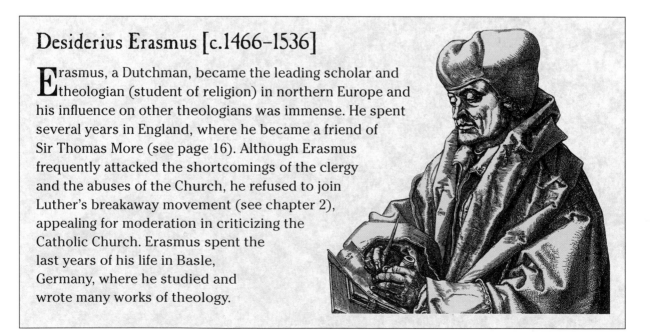

Erasmus, a Dutchman, became the leading scholar and theologian (student of religion) in northern Europe and his influence on other theologians was immense. He spent several years in England, where he became a friend of Sir Thomas More (see page 16). Although Erasmus frequently attacked the shortcomings of the clergy and the abuses of the Church, he refused to join Luther's breakaway movement (see chapter 2), appealing for moderation in criticizing the Catholic Church. Erasmus spent the last years of his life in Basle, Germany, where he studied and wrote many works of theology.

To many people, the holy and simple life led by Christ and his Apostles as told in the Gospels, contrasted sharply with the riches and power of the Church that they saw around them. Monasteries grew rich on money donated by pilgrims, and by grants of land – often bequeathed by wealthy people on their deathbeds, desperately hoping to get to heaven after leading wicked lives. Cardinals and bishops, too, often led lives of great luxury.

The poet Petrarch wrote as early as 1340:

> 'I am living in the Babylon of the West, where cardinals and bishops feast at licentious [immoral] banquets and ride on snow-white horses decked in gold, fed on gold, soon to be shod in gold, if the Lord does not check this slavish luxury.'

The popes were no better, scolded the poet:

> 'It is woeful to see the successors of the poor fishermen of Galilee now loaded with gold and clad in purple.'

Monks were supposed to be celibate, but as this fifteenth-century picture shows, many clearly were not!

Indeed, some popes, such as the notorious Borgia (Pope Alexander VI) and his family, acted little differently from ordinary princes, even to the extent of waging war on their neighbours. It is hardly surprising that the lower ranks of the clergy were also affected by the examples of their leaders. Clergy kept mistresses (they were supposed to be celibate), took bribes, and neglected their work.

> 'In the feast of St Bridget, whosoever will come to the said monastery, devoutly there visiting the Holy Virgin St Bridget, and giving some alms to the sustenance of the same monastery, shall have pardon and clean remission of sins.'

An 'advertisement' from the monastery of Syon in Middlesex, in 1503.

However, the abuses of the Church were by no means the only cause for the coming split. Corruption had always existed. But the Church's failures and refusal to reform itself made it very insecure in the changing world of the sixteenth century. People were beginning to ask questions. Were priests, penances, pilgrimages – even the mass – really necessary to attain salvation and enter heaven?

2

The Reformation

Martin Luther, a German monk, was the person most responsible for the break-away from the Roman Catholic Church and the establishment of Protestant Churches.

The man who lit the spark that was ultimately to divide the Christian Church into Catholics and Protestants was Martin Luther, a monk from Wittenberg in Germany. Like many religious men of his day, Luther was tormented by the idea of his own salvation. If God was all powerful, as the teachings of the Church preached, then surely He must know already who was to be damned and who was to be saved? (This idea is known as predestination.) Yet this contrasted with other teachings of the Church which said that humans, through their own actions of free will – such as giving money to a monastery or going on a pilgrimage – could obtain salvation.

After much study and wrestling with his conscience, Luther came to believe that it was only through complete faith in the mercy of God that people could be forgiven their sins. This doctrine became known as 'Justification by Faith Alone' and was to become the core of Protestant ideas.

Luther questioned many of the concepts of the medieval Church. He believed that people should try to make personal contact with God. They did not need the Pope or priests to do this for them. Nor did they need statues or images, penances or pilgrimages to help them worship. Instead, Luther argued, Christians should look only to the Bible for guidance. The clergy's role should now be to preach to their congregations and explain the holy texts in an understandable way to those who could not read. In this way each person could be his or her own priest and interpret the word of God in their own way.

Luther's ideas were not new. Indeed, St Augustine had preached on the theme of predestination as early as the fourth century AD. However, the time was now ripe for Luther's ideas to take hold. The new spirit of inquiry emerging in the early sixteenth century was accompanied by a period of great religious revival. More and more people were attending church services, buying prayer books and paying priests to say masses for their souls. In this period of greater religious awareness, people were bound to be more critical if they saw abuses in the Church. They were also more likely to listen to new ideas.

With the aid of the printing presses, Luther's pamphlets spread rapidly throughout Germany and beyond. Less than twenty years after Luther's stand, in 1517 (see below), people in central Europe were divided between Protestants and Catholics. The Lutheran (Protestant) Church maintained the traditional Catholic structure of bishops and clergy. Luther also retained the accepted form of worship, which was centred around the mass and the offering of bread and wine – although he denied that these were mystically transformed into the body and blood of Christ. Above all, Luther had no intention of disrupting the social order of lords and peasants. He had no sympathy with the peasants of Germany who rose in revolt against their oppressors in 1524. In this way he won over many of the German princes, who then reformed the Church in their states.

Martin Luther [1483–1546]

Luther studied religion at Wittenberg University, and on a visit to Rome he was shocked to see the corruption of the papal court. He was enraged by the sale of indulgences issued by Pope Leo X, to raise money to rebuild the Church of St Peter in Rome. Indulgences were pieces of paper offering pardon of sins and promises of an entrance to heaven for the purchaser. Luther was so angry that, on 31 October 1517, he nailed a list of ninety-five theses (written statements) to the door of his local church at Wittenberg, attacking the sale of indulgences. His actions challenged the entire structure of the Catholic Church.

In 1521 Emperor Charles V summoned Luther to a special court to argue the case for Protestantism.

The invention of the printing press resulted in a rapid and far-reaching spread of information throughout Europe.

However, Luther's ideas bred other, more revolutionary ideas, and many different sects (groups) broke away from the original movement, setting up their own churches. These breakaway groups within the Protestant movement all wanted to change society, rejecting those with property and privilege, refusing to pay taxes, and sharing goods amongst themselves. To the authorities, both Catholic and moderate Protestant alike, such views were terrifying, and sects such as the Anabaptists (an extreme Protestant group) were brutally persecuted. Such revolutionary ideas were to have a fertile breeding ground in England during the civil wars of the seventeenth century (see chapter 8).

England had a long tradition of criticism of the medieval Church and its popes. One of the most influential of early reformers was a fourteenth-century scholar, John Wycliffe (1320–84). In his book *On Civil Authority*, Wycliffe had outlined almost exactly the same ideas as Luther.

This English anti-Catholic propaganda picture depicts the Pope and his bishops as evil wolves, leading the people by the nose (bottom left) towards the devil (top right). Protestant 'godly men' (top left) are trying to hold back the Pope.

Wycliffe was preaching the Protestant message in England 150 years before Luther.

John Wycliffe [1320–84]

As early as the fourteenth century an Englishman was voicing similar ideas to those of Martin Luther. Wycliffe did not believe that priests were necessary to act as mediators between people and God, and thought the Church should play no part in civil government. He criticized the worldliness of the clergy and produced the first translation of the Bible in English. His followers were nicknamed 'Lollards' – meaning babblers – because they preached so much. They were widely persecuted, although some groups survived until the sixteenth century.

The new spirit of inquiry was also strong in England – indeed Erasmus (see page 8) spent much of his time there. Merchants trading with Germany and the Netherlands brought back more revolutionary ideas. By the 1520s, a group of scholars were meeting regularly at the White Horse Tavern in Cambridge to discuss the new Protestant reforms. This group gave their support to a country priest called William Tyndale, who printed the first English Bible in Germany (1525). Copies of his translation were smuggled into Britain in bales of cloth.

However, there was little sign amongst ordinary people of hatred towards the Catholic Church. Indeed, just as in Germany and other northern European countries, there was a religious revival in England. Wills made around this time show English people leaving money to their village churches. For example, a poor woman called Etheldreda Swan from Cambridgeshire left her entire fortune of 18 shillings (90p) towards the upkeep of her parish church and for candles to be lit for her soul.

3

The King's Reformation

If you look at any British coin today, you can read the letters F.D. stamped on it. These initials stand for *Fidei Defensor*, meaning 'Defender of the Faith'. The title was granted to King Henry VIII by Pope Leo X in 1521, as a reward for a book he wrote which condemned the new religious (Protestant) teachings.

In fact, although Henry was the key figure in the English Reformation, he was not interested in Protestant ideas. Indeed, he burnt Protestants as well as Catholics during his reign. Henry's reasons for bringing about a break with Rome and founding the Church of England were a mixture of convenience and greed.

Henry had married Catherine of Aragon, the widow of his dead brother in 1509, but unfortunately for her, she was only able to produce a daughter, Princess Mary. For Henry, a male heir was vital to ensure the succession of the Tudor family. He was haunted by fears of a renewal of the Wars of the Roses of the previous century – struggles for the throne between the rival houses (families) of York and Lancaster, which had torn England apart. He was also in love with one of his wife's attendants, Anne Boleyn, and wished to make her his queen as soon as possible.

Henry had appointed Cardinal Wolsey as Lord Chancellor and, as he needed the Pope to grant him a divorce, he asked Wolsey to make the necessary arrangements. In normal circumstances this would not have been a problem, but the Pope was having his own political difficulties at the time, and so he dithered over granting the King's request. Henry lost patience. He dismissed Wolsey, who had failed to get the required results. Summoning Parliament, he instructed its members to pass the Act of Supremacy (1534), ending the powers of the Pope, and appointed himself as 'Supreme Head of the Church in England'.

A portrait of Henry VIII by Hans Holbein. The King, unintentionally, set the English Reformation in motion.

Cardinal Thomas Wolsey (1471–1530) was Henry VIII's Lord Chancellor at the time of his divorce from Catherine of Aragon.

By the Act of Supremacy Henry could now run the Church as he liked. By 1533 he had divorced Catherine and married Anne Boleyn. One of the few men who opposed these changes was Henry's old friend Sir Thomas More; he was executed for his opposition.

Between 1536 and 1539, Henry closed all the monasteries in England and Wales – an act known as the Dissolution of the Monasteries. Because the loyalty of most monks was to the Pope, they threatened Henry's power. But more importantly, the monasteries were immensely rich, and Henry needed their wealth to pay for his wars in France and to build an English fleet. As a result of the Dissolution Henry gained vast lands belonging to the monasteries, which he sold to nobles and rich members of the gentry.

To begin with there was little opposition among the ruling classes and, indeed, some priests to Henry's policies. But not everyone was in favour of the selling off and plundering

This print shows a triumphant Henry VIII trampling on Pope Clement VII, after declaring himself head of the Church in England.

16

of the monasteries. Many people were bewildered and upset at the closing of religious buildings which had long been important providers of charity and shelter for the poor and sick. This was particularly true in the north, where in 1536, a huge uprising known as the Pilgrimage of Grace began gathering to oppose the King's reforms. Henry dispersed the uprising by making promises he then did not keep. The Pilgrimage's leader, Robert Aske, and other leaders were executed, and the uprising fizzled out. But it was a warning of many other such revolts that were to occur during the sixteenth century.

The ruins of Rievaulx Abbey in Yorkshire. Such ruins exist all over England, and are a haunting reminder of how magnificent the abbeys must have been before the Dissolution.

However, Henry's Reformation (known as the Henrician Reformation) introduced only limited changes to the doctrines and services of the Catholic Church. Henry had thrown off the power of the Pope, dissolved the monasteries and decreed that a new English Bible should be read in churches, but his Act of the Six Articles (doctrines which governed the new Church), passed by Parliament in 1539, was still essentially Catholic.

During the reign of Henry's son, Edward VI (1547–53), Protestantism was more firmly imposed on the country. Because Edward was only a child when he came to the throne, England was ruled by his powerful Protestant relations. In 1549 an Act of Uniformity was passed. This imposed the new form of worship, as outlined in Archbishop Cranmer's Book of Common Prayer, on all churches. This prayerbook contains some of the most beautiful writing in the English language and is still used by the Anglican Church today.

Attempts were also made to change the interiors of churches to make them look plainer. Images were pulled down and holy pictures on the walls of churches were painted over and the Ten Commandments written up in their place. 'All altars were pulled down and every speaker spoke against all images' wrote a Protestant commentator. He may have been exaggerating, but it probably reflects the trend. A second Act of Uniformity was passed in 1552, which made it compulsory to attend church on Sundays.

All this was very bewildering to many people. Two rebellions during Edward's reign, one of them Catholic and one Protestant, reflect the divisions in the country at the time. Rebels in the West Country, clinging to the traditions of the past, declared: 'We will have the mass in Latin as before,

Thomas Cranmer was the pioneering Protestant Archbishop under both Henry VIII and Edward VI. He was burnt at the stake for his Protestant beliefs during the reign of Queen Mary (see page 23).

18

The cover of the new English Bible. The King is shown at the top handing copies of the Bible to Archbishop Cranmer and Lord Chancellor Thomas Cromwell.

and celebrated by the priest without any man or woman communicating with him'. They also complained bitterly about the loss of altars which in the past would have housed the sacrament of the mass. By contrast, a Protestant rebellion in Norfolk, led by Robert Kett, condemned the decline in the competence of priests, indicating the general confusion of the times, when people did not know what to believe. Kett demanded that 'Priests or vicars that be not able to preach and set forth the word of God to their parishioners may therefore be put from his parish (sent away) and the people there to choose another…'

4

Counter Reformation & Compromise

Queen Mary, sometimes known as 'Bloody Mary', dedicated her reign to returning England to the Catholic religion.

Following the death of Edward VI, Henry VIII's eldest daughter the Catholic Princess Mary, succeeded to the throne. Mary was determined to restore the Roman Catholic religion in England. The traditional picture portrayed of Mary's reign (1553–59) is of persecutions and burnings of the Protestant martyrs of the new religion. Her name has gone down in history as 'Bloody Mary'.

The Protestant chronicler (writer), John Foxe, recorded a moving conversation that took place between a guard (Master Wingfield) and a Protestant martyr (John Kerby), as he was taken to be burnt at Ipswich:

> Master Wingfield said to Kerby: *'Remember the fire is hot, take heed of thine enterprise, that thou take no more upon thee than thou shalt be able to perform. The terror is great, the pain will be extreme, and life is sweet. Better it were betimes to stick to mercy, while there is still hope of life, than rashly begin to shrink.'*

> To whom Kerby answered: *'Ah, Master Wingfield! Be at my burning and you shall say, there standeth a Christian soldier in the fire. For I know that fire and water, sword and all other things are in the hands of God, and he will suffer no more to be laid on us than we can bear.'*

Mary had a tragic and unhappy life. As the only child of Henry VIII and his first wife, Catherine of Aragon, she was adored by her father as a child, only to fall abruptly from favour when her mother was divorced. She was humiliated by Henry, declared illegitimate by Act of Parliament, and compelled to act as lady-in-waiting to her baby half-sister Elizabeth. (Elizabeth's glory did not last long. She too was declared illegitimate, when at the age of three, her mother,

Ye fhalbe led before Princes and rulers for my names fake. *Math. 10.*

This print shows Protestants, both men and women, roped together to be marched from Colchester, in Norfolk, to London, where they were to be burnt on bonfires.

Anne Boleyn, was executed). As Mary told her little sister, seventeen years her junior: 'It is your turn now to learn to be silent, as I have done.'

Mary had always been a sincere Catholic. She would have nothing to do with the new ideas introduced by her father and brother. Her main aim on coming to the throne was to return England to the Roman Catholic Church, and it was for this reason that a number of Protestant lords attempted to put her little cousin, Lady Jane Grey, on the throne in her place. But the country would have none of it. A series of rebellions was crushed, and poor Lady Jane, who was still a child and never wanted to be queen, was beheaded.

Mary was now free to return her country to the 'old religion'. It is doubtful if the majority of people objected much to this provided the nobility and gentry, who had gained church lands after the Dissolution of the Monasteries, were allowed to keep them. On this condition Parliament agreed to undo the Protestant reforms of previous reigns and bring England back into the Catholic fold.

But by now the quarrel between Catholic and Protestant was becoming an international struggle. France was torn by religious wars which were to come to a head in the Massacre of St Bartholomew's Eve in 1572, when 15,000 Protestants were slaughtered in Paris in one night. The Pope issued a special medal to commemorate the event.

In Spain, the most powerful Catholic nation in Europe, the dreaded medieval Inquisition was brought back to preserve the Catholic Church. The Inquisition's purpose was to punish heretics by burning them alive. It was believed by all religious groups at this time, that the only way to cleanse someone who disagreed with the teachings of the Church – whether Catholic or Protestant – was to burn them. In Spain, heretics were sentenced to death and burned alive at ceremonies known as auto-da-fés (acts of faith). (Recently it has been suggested that the activities of the Inquisition were exaggerated for Protestant propaganda purposes, and that there were fewer victims of the Inquisition than had previously been thought.)

However, when Mary decided to marry King Philip II of Spain many English people were appalled. Were these same dreadful ceremonies and burnings to take place in England?

An auto-da-fé carried out by the Spanish Inquisition. In these ceremonies heretics were dressed in ceremonial clothes, with tall yellow hats, and were burnt on bonfires in front of large crowds.

Protestant women being 'cleansed' by burning. A devil is depicted fleeing from one of the victim's mouths.

At their wedding ceremony at Westminster Abbey, Philip was pelted with dead dogs and rotting vegetables. And Mary's critics were right, for in 1555 persecution began against the Protestants. Around a thousand Protestant preachers fled abroad to Switzerland, where they were able to study the doctrines of the French Protestant reformer, John Calvin (see page 26).

Some three hundred Protestant martyrs – mainly from the south-east – were burnt, including the intensely Protestant preachers Hugh Latimer, and Nicolas Ridley. The most famous martyr was Archbishop Cranmer, who had been the Protestant Archbishop in the reigns of both Henry VIII and Edward VI (see page 18).

Thomas Cranmer [1489–1556]

Cranmer was the first Protestant Archbishop of Canterbury during the reigns of Henry VIII and his son Edward VI. When the Catholic Queen Mary succeeded to the throne, Cranmer renounced all the new (Protestant) teachings. But then he changed his mind. He reaffirmed his Protestant beliefs, and was sentenced to be burnt. His last words were: 'For as much as my hand offended in writing contrary to my heart, my hand therefore shall be the first to be punished; for when I come to the fire it shall be the first to be burnt.'

This painting of musicians decorates the walls of a castle in Yorkshire. Puritan disapproval of activities such as music, acting and dancing were not allowed to influence Elizabethan life.

After Mary's death in 1558, her sister Elizabeth became queen. Elizabeth's attitude to the religious excesses of previous reigns can be summed up in her words: 'I do not wish to make windows in men's souls'. The religious settlement of 1559 was designed to overcome hostility to a Protestant Church that really did not quite know what it had been doing for the past thirty years. In the countryside people were bewildered. They were always being told to believe in something different. The most striking example was that of priests being told at one minute that they could marry, then they could not, and then suddenly, they could again – these changes were very confusing for all concerned.

Elizabeth herself was not particularly religious. She had seen far too much religion under her father, brother and sister to want to go down the same fanatical road. She had been imprisoned in the Tower of London for over a year during Mary's reign, and just missed being executed (the Spanish ambassador, indeed, insisted that she should be and it was only Mary's kindness and Elizabeth's ready wit that saved her).

So Elizabeth's 1559 religious settlement was moderate and designed to be accepted by as many people as possible. Cranmer's Book of Common Prayer was brought back and the Pope's authority again denied. The Anglican Church was to be a 'middle of the road' Church. The churches kept their altars, the priests their robes, and people continued to enjoy themselves on Sundays.

This did not satisfy everyone. The Catholics naturally disliked it intensely – at this time half the nobility and the majority of the people were still basically Catholic. There were plots, particularly centred around Mary, Queen of Scots (see also page 30), imprisoned in England for the last twenty years of her life. She was eventually executed in 1587 – very reluctantly by her cousin Elizabeth, who pretended she did not know which document she was putting her name to when she signed the death warrant.

But the Scottish queen's execution was probably necessary. Things were on the move in Europe. In 1570, Queen Elizabeth had been excommunicated (expelled from the Church) by the Pope, who declared that her subjects should no longer obey her. A year after the death of Mary, Queen of Scots, a Spanish fleet (the Armada) set sail to invade England (1588), and was defeated. The Spanish aim was to depose Elizabeth and bring back Catholicism in England. All branches of the Protestant religion could unite in opposing this aim. The attempted invasion and numerous plots to restore Catholicism led to a hardening of attitudes and some persecution of Catholics.

The other religious group who disliked Elizabeth's religious settlement were the Puritans. One chronicler described these as 'the hotter sort of Protestants'. (You can read more about Puritans in the next chapter.) They were strong in Parliament, and keen to turn England into a more 'godly' society. But with the continual threat from Spain, they were never prepared to push their views to outright opposition.

A portrait of Elizabeth I. The Queen believed in moderation in religious matters, but she had to tread warily. By now, the divisions between Catholics and Protestants had become an issue involving powerful nations in Europe.

Mary, Queen of Scots [1542–87]

Mary became Queen of Scotland when only a baby. She was married to the French king, Francis II, but after his early death she returned to Scotland and married her cousin Lord Darnley, and later the Earl of Bothwell, who was thought to have murdered Darnley. She was forced to give up her throne in favour of her son, who became James VI of Scotland and later James I of England. In 1568 she fled to England where she was imprisoned. Mary had a claim to the English throne and she became the centre of Catholic plots against Queen Elizabeth, who eventually ordered her execution. She was beheaded at Fotheringhay Castle in Northamptonshire, on 8th February 1587.

5

John Calvin and Puritanism

In 1536 a young Frenchman called John Calvin arrived in Geneva, Switzerland. Although he was only a child when Luther was making his historic break with Rome (see chapter 2), he was deeply affected by Luther's ideas. During his time in Geneva Calvin was to take Luther's ideas one step further. Indeed by the time of his death in 1564 he had transformed Geneva into the strict, God-fearing government which was to become the model for all Puritan reformers throughout Europe.

For Calvin, the whole point of Christianity meant the absolute supremacy of God. He went much further than Luther in his emphasis on the importance of predestination (see page 10). Calvin wrote:

'We call predestination God's eternal decree, by which He determined what He willed of to become of each man. For all are not created in equal condition; rather eternal life is ordained [ordered] for some, eternal damnation for others.'

John Calvin founded the most extreme form of Protestantism. After living for years in danger of arrest because of his views, he finally settled in Switzerland. Calvin taught that people should live strict, God-fearing lives, and that pleasure was sinful.

Calvin put these ideas into practice by re-organizing the Church in Geneva. Calvinist ministers were no longer appointed by bishops but were elected by their congregations. Calvin also introduced the idea of church elders, who were usually individuals chosen from the congregations. They, like the ministers, had power to control and regulate the lives of ordinary people. Sin, as ministers judged it, now became a crime. Adultery, failure to attend church, playing sports on Sundays, swearing, gambling, dancing, drinking were all forbidden. Punishments were severe, and included fines, beatings and even execution.

Calvinism encouraged effort, industry, study and a sense of purpose. These qualities made the religion popular with the rich, including merchants and some of the aristocracy. Here was a movement that did not threaten the existing order. And here was the birth of the 'Protestant work ethic' (meaning that work leads to godliness).

The caption for this sixteenth-century cartoon runs as follows: 'Nick Froth, the tapster (publican), and Rule Roast the cook, are complaining against the Puritan Sunday and the "constraint lately set forth against drinking, betting and piping on the Sabbath Day, and against selling meate."'

With the printing presses hard at work, and travel across borders relatively easy, Calvin's ideas spread far and wide across Europe. They had certainly reached England by Edward VI's reign, and were the reason for some of the more revolutionary reforms that took place when he was on the throne.

The persecuted Protestants during Mary's reign had all fled to Geneva. When Elizabeth became queen they came back to England with new enthusiasm, hoping to set up 'a more godly society'.

We have an image of Puritans as stern men and women, in tall hats and plain black clothes, disapproving of anyone who seemed to be enjoying themselves: no Christmas festivities (only prayers), no fun on Sundays, no dancing or sport – only work and sermons. But there is another side to Puritans. Many of them were egalitarians – they believed in equality, that one good man (or woman) was the same as another.

Queen Elizabeth's Secretary of State, Francis Walsingham, who was not a Puritan, wrote:

> *'Poverty was an eyesore to every man, therefore the Puritans put it into the people's heads that if discipline was planted, there should be no vagabonds nor beggars: a thing very plausible'.*

6

Calvinism in Scotland

On the last day of February, 1528, Patrick Hamilton was burnt at the stake outside the University of St Andrews. 'A winter gale blew the smoke across the faces of those who watched, and the reek of his burning infected them all', wrote an onlooker. Patrick Hamilton was Scotland's first Reformation martyr. When the Reformation did come to Scotland it was to put the practices of John Calvin into place more firmly than in any other country in Europe.

Scotland, more than most countries, had cause to hate the Catholic Church. Catholics owned more than half the land there. Priests were idle, and wandering friars toured the country demanding money for services which should have been free.

A poet of the time, John of the Common Weal, wrote how people 'groaned under the extortions of great fat friars', who he described in very unflattering terms (see over).

Mary, Queen of Scots (1542–87). This sad but romantic queen made many mistakes, and paid for them with her life.

John Knox [c.1513–72]

Knox was a Scotsman, born in East Lothian. He became a Catholic priest and later joined a Protestant group after one of his friends was burnt at the stake as a heretic. When Mary, Queen of Scots came to the throne, Knox fled to Geneva, where he worked with Calvin. He returned to Scotland in 1559, where he rallied the Scottish reformers with his preaching. The establishment of the Presbyterian Church of Scotland is almost entirely due to the work of John Knox.

[They] labour not and are well fed
I mean, not labouring spiritually
Lying in dens like idle dogs
I compare them to well fed hogs.

The Scots were eager to follow the reformation that had occurred in England under Henry VIII. But after the death of their king, James V, in 1542, they had an infant queen who was later to become Queen of France. Having been brought up at the French court, Mary, Queen of Scots was a Catholic (see also page 25).

In 1557, the Protestant leaders in Scotland signed a covenant (agreement) to defend 'the most blessed Word of God and his Congregation'. Helped by the fiery sermons of the preacher John Knox and support from the English, a Calvinist, Presbyterian Church was established in most of Scotland. The arrival of Mary, a Catholic Queen, did not do anything to change the establishment of the Presbyterian Church. She did not change her religion (despite bloodthirsty lectures from John Knox which made her cry). Her whirlwind six-year reign has become one of the enduring romances of British history, but it changed very little.

John Knox lecturing Mary, Queen of Scots at her Palace of Holyrood.

7

The Road to Civil War

Although James VI of Scotland and I of England was an odd, shambling figure, who had favourites, he was also a shrewd and learned man. James was the son of Mary, Queen of Scots. He had spent his youth being carted around from one bleak Scottish castle to another, as rival lords fought to keep him in power. He was also brought up by strict Presbyterians, whom he detested.

James succeeded Elizabeth I on the English throne in 1603. He was delighted by all he saw in England, and very glad to leave the misty glens and warring Scottish nobles behind him. He liked the moderate Church of England set up by Elizabeth I. In a famous comment made to a Bishop, he said 'No bishop, no king, no nobility'. He understood that the three stood or fell together. And this was very wise of him, for that is exactly what was to happen in the turmoil of the civil wars of the 1640s. The bishops were abolished in 1642, the king (Charles I) was executed in 1649 and the House of Lords was abolished a year later.

Although agreeing with the ceremonies and forms of worship of the Church of England, James hoped to get agreement between differing churchmen. Consequently, a few months after coming to the throne, he summoned all sections of the clergy to a conference 'to hear and see and listen to one another'. The conference failed to bring the divided groups of Puritans and moderates together, but it did produce a new 'Authorized' or 'King James Version' of the Bible.

Tyndale, as we have read in chapter 2, produced the first printed Bible in English. Several more Bibles were produced after that, but none of them was quite satisfactory. Now, forty-seven scholars were commissioned to make a new translation from the original Greek and Hebrew. James himself not only took a great interest in the work, but also

Although he was often considered to be a fool, James I was a great deal wiser than he seemed. He was nicknamed 'the wisest fool in Christendom'.

The Gunpowder Plot

In 1605 Catholic plotters planned to destroy England's Protestant ruling class by blowing up King James and the Houses of Parliament with all the lords and members. The plot was discovered and the conspirators were tortured and then executed. For centuries to come, memories of the

The conspirators in the Gunpowder Plot. Guido (Guy) Fawkes, the best-known plotter, is third from the right.

'Gunpowder Plot' as it became known, were to stir up a violent hatred of Catholics among many English people. Anglicans who used elaborate religious ceremonies in their worship were suspected of being secret Catholics, and fear of 'popery' was a powerful influence on English politics for centuries.

in the translation itself. The new translation was issued in 1611, after seven years of work. To many, King James' Bible is still regarded as 'the noblest monument of English prose'.

By the Act of Supremacy, in 1533, Henry VIII had demolished one authority which everyone understood – that of the pope. Kings would now take on the burden of 'divine' responsibility, and should not be challenged by their lawful subjects. As the ruler of England, Scotland and Ireland, King James had a deep-rooted belief in his 'divine' responsibility (The Divine Right of Kings).

> *'The state of monarchy is the supremest thing on Earth. For kings are not only God's lieutenants upon Earth and sit upon God's throne, but even by God Himself they are called gods.'*

This was a disastrous policy to pursue at the beginning of the seventeenth century. With so many new ideas flying about, who in their right minds would believe in a divinely-inspired ruler who could do whatever he wished; tax people as he liked or make them change their religion?

This painting of Charles I, by Anthony van Dyck, shows the King in all his splendour as 'God's annointed on Earth' (appointed by God). In fact Charles was a small, shy man with a slight stammer. He made up for these defects however, with a great sense of his own dignity.

Unfortunately, James's son Charles I took up this idea of Divine Right even more strongly than his father. Charles, who came to the throne after his father's death in 1629, was certainly deeply attached to the Church of England. He had been brought up to respect and love its doctrines and teachings. But he had no sympathy at all with Puritans.

In his dislike of Puritans Charles found an ally in Bishop William Laud, whom he created Archbishop of Canterbury. Laud was determined to free England and Scotland of Puritanism, and together they tried to impose the 'Laudian Church', with its use of rites and ceremonies, on the English and later the Scots.

This cartoon shows the Archbishop of Canterbury, William Laud, being served with the ears of the three Puritan preachers Bastwicke, Burton and Prynne.

Puritans who disapproved of the 'Laudian Church' were persecuted. In the most famous case of persecution, three Puritan preachers, Bastwicke, Burton and Prynne, were sentenced to have their ears cut off and be put in the stocks, to be mocked by the public. But the punishment backfired. The victims were able to preach to large and sympathetic crowds, who regarded them as martyrs against the King and his hated archbishop.

However, what really infuriated Puritans was Charles' attitude towards Catholics. He appeared to let them do as they liked, while he stamped on the Puritans. He married a French Catholic Princess, Henrietta Maria, who had a great influence over the King and a large Catholic following at court. Charles, in fact, never dabbled with Catholicism, and he repeated his life-long support of the Church of England minutes before he died on the scaffold (see pages 39–40). But, if Charles had trouble convincing his English subjects of his good intentions, he was in for a nasty shock when he tried to impose his religious ideas on the Scots.

In 1637, Charles ordered a new Anglican prayer book to be read in churches throughout Scotland. When a trembling bishop began to read the service in Scotland's principal church of Saint Giles in Edinburgh, he was met with yells and catcalls. Then one large fishwife got up and threw her stool at the bishop and a riot took place. Similar acts of violence occurred throughout Scotland.

The Scots were furious that anyone should try to tell them what they should or should not believe. Crowds from all classes of society flocked to sign the 'Covenant', as it became known, which supported the Calvinist Church in Scotland. They also began to train an army.

Taken by surprise at the extent of the outcry, Charles was nevertheless determined to crush all opposition. But as he had decided to rule without Parliament for eleven years, he was woefully short of money to fight a war. His inadequate forces were easily defeated by the Scots.

This was the spark that was to set off the Civil War. Charles had got himself into a mess. He now had to call Parliament in order to raise some money. But this – known as the 'Short Parliament' – was not a success. Why should Charles be given money when he seemed to be favouring Catholics at home, using his navy to help the Spanish in the Netherlands, and making war on his Protestant Scottish subjects? The King dissolved Parliament within a month.

Charles then went personally to Scotland to try and calm matters – without much success. While playing golf on the links at Glasgow, the King received another shattering piece of news – Ireland had exploded into rebellion. According to onlookers, Charles did not bat an eyelid and carried on to win his game of golf. But he was not to win the game in England.

An English print made in 1638. It shows 'Jock the Scotsman' handing Charles I a petition asking him to repeal (cancel) the religious decrees he had imposed on Scotland.

This cartoon, dating from the Civil War, shows the 'true' preacher adressing the well-behaved churchgoers (left), while out in the open a 'false' preacher, (one not belonging to the Church of England), stirs up the unruly crowd.

The Orthodox true Minifter,   the Seducer and falfe Prophet.

The King needed an army to crush the Irish (although they were rebelling quite justifiably against Protestant settlers who were driving them from their lands). The new Parliament that he was forced to call (known as the 'Long Parliament' because it lasted from 1642 to 1651) was in no mind to grant the King's request. Rightly, Parliament, led by John Pym, feared that Charles would use any new forces he raised to crush them first. So here was the crunch – who was to command the army and the money? Not Charles, was Parliament's answer. A Grand Remonstrance (protest) was prepared in Parliament, condemning all abuses that the King had committed during his reign. Charles, it was said, was unfit to appoint his own ministers or have control over the armed forces.

For Charles, the last insult was when his beloved Queen, Henrietta Maria was accused of being a traitor. Having made a bungled attempt to capture his opponents in the House of Commons, he missed them as they escaped out of a back door into a leaky barge which wobbled down the Thames. 'All my birds have flown', sighed Charles.

He left his capital the next day, never to see it again till just before he was executed. He set up his standard (flag) at Nottingham, where it promptly fell down in a storm: not a good omen.

8

Civil War

Nobody in England really wanted war. In the country-side the split between King and Parliament was greeted with dismay. In twenty-four counties the gentry agreed among themselves not to take sides, and so would not have to fight their fellow countrymen. Some people, known as 'clubmen', joined together to stop either army – Royalist or Parliamentarian – destroying their lands.

The English Civil War – or what should be more accurately called the 'British Civil War' – as Scots, Irish and Welsh were deeply involved, had many underlying causes. But all historians are agreed that religion played an important part – if not the most important part in causing the war.

To begin with both sides held back. The first major battle – at Edgehill on 23 October, 1642 – was a drawn affair. Nobody won, but the Royalists could certainly have marched on London if they had wanted to. Charles did not want to. He was horrified by the loss of life.

When Edward Verney, a moderate Parliamentarian, joined the King he wrote

> 'For my part I do not like the quarrel, and do
> heartily wish the King would yield and consent to
> what they demand. I have taken up arms from
> personal loyalty. I have eaten the King's bread and
> served him near thirty years and will not do so base
> a thing as to forsake him; and rather choose to
> lose my life, which I am sure I shall do.'

Verney did die. He was killed bravely defending the Royal Standard at Edgehill. Like many, he perhaps only half believed in what he was doing.

As Sir William Waller, a Parliamentary General wrote to his old friend Sir Ralph Hopton, a Royalist General 'I detest this war without an enemy...'

Oliver Cromwell rose from discontented, middle-aged country squire, to be one of the greatest of English military leaders and the ruler of Britain. However, he was never able to settle the religious differences of his unruly countrymen.

General Fairfax, leading the Parliamentary forces, celebrates his victory at the Battle of Naseby (1645). Through this final, crushing defeat, Charles I lost his last chance of retaining his kingdom as he wanted it.

In 1643 the King was definitely winning the war. His dashing cavalry general, Prince Rupert, was winning battle after battle. Parliament had to do something to stop this. Parliamentary leaders made an alliance with the Scots in 1644, and with the help of the Scots army the Royalists were decisively defeated at the battle of Marston Moor. To keep the Scots as allies, Parliament had to agree to establish a Presbyterian (Calvinist) Church in England. This was resented by many English people, who felt that worshipping in a strict Presbyterian Church was as bad as a Laudian Church (see pages 33 and 34).

The champion of the Parliamentary side was Oliver Cromwell. Having been a farmer and politician for most of his life, in his middle age he became the most successful cavalry general of the seventeenth century. Cromwell won the war for Parliament. He had built up an army from the common people and turned it into an effective fighting force. He belonged to a small religious group called the Independents, and he was very much a Puritan, who thanked God for all his victories – of which there were many.

> *'An absolute victory obtained by the Lord's blessing... We never charged, but we routed the enemy. The left wing which I commanded, being our horse – saving a few Scots in the rear – beat all the Prince's horse. God made them as stubble to our swords.'*
>
> Oliver Cromwell, after defeating Prince Rupert at the Battle of Marston Moor, 1644.

Oliver Cromwell called for religious freedom for those with 'tender consciences' and warned that his men had not fought so hard only to have the Presbyterian religion forced upon them by the Scots. He got his way. In three smashing victories, he beat the Scots at Preston and Dunbar (1650) and later Worcester (1651).

Charles I had sought refuge with the Scots after his defeat at the Battle of Naseby in 1645. He was handed over to Cromwell's army in 1647 and was put on trial and convicted of treason against the people. On 30 January 1649, Charles was executed in London.

At his trial in 1647, Charles I showed more quiet sincerity and dignity than he had ever shown during his reign.

As the axe fell to behead the King, a boy of seventeen would remember as long as he lived the sound that rose from the watching crowd; 'such a groan as I never heard before, and desire I may never hear again.'

Just before he was beheaded, Charles I declared:

> *'I die a Christian according to the profession of the Church of England, as I found it left me by my father... I have a good Cause and I have a gracious God; I will say no more.'*

Meanwhile England had become a republic, known as the Commonwealth. Cromwell gradually took over the reins as ruler, but having won the war, he could not win the peace. Many different religious and political ideas had begun to circulate in the climate of freedom produced by the war. There were groups such as the Levellers, who wanted political equality for everyone and others who declared the second coming of Christ was about to happen.

Cromwell survived – just. He summoned a Parliament of 'All the Saints' (religious men similar to himself), but that did not work either. Finally he was appointed Lord Protector and he ruled the country through his 'major generals'. He died in 1658 and was succeeded by his son Richard, who soon gave up and civil war again threatened. General Monck, commanding a parliamentary army in Scotland, marched south to take control. He invited Charles I's eldest son to return from exile as King Charles II.

9

Moderation and the Age of Reason

THE KING
&Equeries
Gentlemen Penſioners & Equeries
Yeomen of the Guard

Charles II was not like his father. He was intelligent and ready to compromise. When he was surprisingly offered back his kingdom, in 1660, he was determined to be moderate, tolerating all branches of the Protestant religion. The Church of England was restored – as were its bishops. But there was no persecution of Puritans, or Dissenters, as Protestants outside the Church of England were now called. However, Dissenters were not allowed to hold government or other important positions, but they were allowed to worship as they wished.

A brief break in this new spirit of moderation occurred when, in 1685, Charles' brother James succeeded him on the throne. James II had become a Catholic and because of this, attempts had been made to prevent him from succeeding to the throne. But Charles had always supported his brother and refused to name anyone else as his successor.

The coronation procession of Charles II in 1660. After the turmoil of the last twenty years, the restoration of the monarch was greeted with relief by most of the population.

James was supported by the majority of the country as the rightful heir to the throne, and he easily defeated a rebellion by the Protestant Duke of Monmouth, Charles II's illegitimate son.

But James then outraged his subjects by his policy of favouring Catholics. He promoted Catholics to important posts in the universities and other positions of power. He also tried to bring back the sort of authoritive rule that his father (Charles I) had believed in. When in 1688, James' Catholic second wife gave birth to a male heir, the English people had had enough. The answer was to call on the Dutch Prince William of Orange and his wife, who were Protestants.

The 'Glorious Revolution' of 1688, which marked the arrival of William and Mary on the throne, was a turning point in British history, establishing moderation in religion and the beginnings of a constitutional monarchy.

William of Orange, a grandson of Charles I, was married to James's oldest daughter, Mary. He was, at the time, desperately trying to defend his native country, Holland, against attacks by the Catholic king of France, Louis XIV. When the English Parliament invited the Prince and his wife to become joint monarchs William was able to bring the English into the war against Louis XIV. James II fled to France, and after landing in Ireland with an army in 1689, he was defeated at the Battle of the Boyne in 1690.

The events of 1688 were a turning point in British history. Called the 'Glorious Revolution', the arrival of William and Mary marked the beginning of a partly constitutional monarchy and a good relationship between monarch and Parliament, which laid the foundations for today's constitutional government. A law was passed that Parliament should be summoned every three years. Parliament now had control over the monarch's purse strings. Dissenters (but not Catholics) were allowed back into public office.

Two men were influential in bringing about the new atmosphere of tolerance. The philosopher John Locke (1632–1704) wrote about peace and reconciliation between king and people. The scientist Isaac Newton (1642–1727) discovered the Laws of Gravity, and so doing changed the way people understood the universe. Both men were devout Christians, but they viewed the world in a different way from the narrow-minded bigots of the last two centuries. The views of these Englishmen had a profound effect on the ideas of the French philosophers Montesquieu, Rousseau and Voltaire. These men came to believe in Humanism – denying traditional religion, but believing in the compassion of humanity.

As the eighteenth century drew on, the Church of England seemed to sleep. John Wesley, a thoughtful and peaceful man, founded the Methodist religion, which was to become a forceful, world-wide Dissenting Church. John and his brother Charles held vast open-air meetings, preaching mainly to the labouring classes, who were finding little comfort in the uninspiring, ritualized services of the Church of England. Methodism began to spread in the eighteenth century; during the following century it was to become a powerful, world-wide religious force.

King George I (1660–1727). By the Act of Settlement of 1701 Parliament ruled that no Catholic could become king or queen of England. When Queen Anne died in 1714, leaving no heirs, her distant relative, the Protestant Prince George of Hanover, succeeded to the throne.

Isaac Newton's scientific discoveries led to a new way of looking at the world in which religious differences were no longer the most important factor.

John Wesley [1703–91]

John Wesley was brought up in the Church of England, but after a spiritual experience he decided to form a religious movement to try to revitalize the Anglican Church. The movement later became a breakaway religion, called Methodism. John and his brother Charles preached their message to huge crowds, gathered at open-air meetings - as Dissenters, the Wesleys could not preach in churches. Their congregations were mainly of men and women from the working classes, who were encouraged by the Wesleys' message to live moral lives. In the nineteenth century, with the growth of the British Empire and the dramatic changes brought about by the Industrial Revolution, Methodism expanded, to become an influential religion all over the world.

John and Charles Wesley held vast open-air meetings; the first one in Bristol was attended by 3,000 people. To the end of his life, John travelled the length and breadth of Britain, sometimes riding 100 km a day, to deliver his sermons.

Meanwhile the Church of England snoozed, waking briefly in the mid-nineteenth century, when two of its prominent members suddenly became Catholics. John Newman and Henry Manning both became cardinals in the Catholic Church, not at all what the Tudor and early Stuart Church of England would have expected.

Time Line

1500–1550

◊ **c.1455** First printing press in use

◊ **1509** Henry VIII becomes king

◊ **1511** Erasmus teaches at Cambridge

◊ **1517** Luther protests against sale of indulgences in Germany

◊ **1521** Luther condemned as a heretic

◊ **1525** First English Bible printed

◊ **1533** Henry VIII divorces Catherine of Aragon

◊ **1534** Act of Supremacy passed

◊ **1536** Calvin establishes Protestant Church in Geneva

◊ **1541** Knox begins Reformation in Scotland

◊ **1547** Edward VI becomes king

◊ **1549** Act of Uniformity; Kett's rebellion

| 1500 | 1510 | 1520 | 1530 | 1540 | 1550 |

1550–1600

◊ **1553** Mary Tudor becomes queen; Catholic Church re-established

◊ **1556** Act of Supremacy repealed

◊ **1558** Elizabeth becomes queen

◊ **1559** Act of Settlement

◊ **1561** Scottish Church established

◊ **1562** Second Act of Uniformity

◊ **1568** Mary, Queen of Scots imprisoned in England

◊ **1570** Pope excommunicates Elizabeth

◊ **1572** Massacre of St Bartholomew in France

◊ **1587** Mary, Queen of Scots executed

◊ **1588** Spanish Armada defeated

| 1550 | 1560 | 1570 | 1580 | 1590 | 1600 |

1600–1650

◊ **1603** James VI of Scotland becomes James I of England

◊ **1605** Gunpowder Plot discovered – leaders executed

◊ **1611** King James Bible published

◊ **1625** Charles I becomes king

◊ **1629** Parliament protests against changes in religion

◊ **1637** Introduction of Anglican prayer book causes riots in Scotland

◊ **1642** Outbreak of Civil War

◊ **1645** Defeat of Royalists by Parliamentary and Scots armies

◊ **1649** Charles I executed

| 1600 | 1610 | 1620 | 1630 | 1640 | 1650 |

1650–1700

◊ **1653** Cromwell appointed Lord Protector

◊ **1660** Charles II restored to the throne

◊ **1685** James II becomes king

◊ **1686** James issues Declaration of Indulgence

◊ **1688** William and Mary invited to become king and queen. Flight of James II

◊ **1689** Bill of Rights passed Toleration Act passed

| 1650 | 1660 | 1670 | 1680 | 1690 | 1700 |

1700–1750

◊ **1702** Accession of Queen Anne

◊ **1707** Act of Union between England, Scotland, Ireland and Wales

◊ **1714** George I succeeds to the throne

◊ **1727** George II becomes king

◊ **1730** John Wesley forms Methodist movement at Oxford

◊ **1739** Methodist movement develops in London

| 1700 | 1710 | 1720 | 1730 | 1740 | 1750 |

Glossary

Abuses Corrupt practices.

Alms Money given to the poor.

Anglican Church Another name for the Church of England.

Bigots Narrow-minded religious people who have no respect for other's opinions.

Calvinism The Protestant Church founded by John Calvin.

Celibate To take a vow of chastity – living without sexual intercourse.

Clergy Men, and sometimes women, who are ordained as ministers of religion.

Congregation The people who regularly gather together to attend church.

Constitutional Relating to the constitution, the fundamental workings of a nation's government.

Counter Reformation The reform movement of the Roman Catholic Church in the sixteenth and seventeenth centuries, formed as a reaction to the Protestant Reformation.

Divine Right The idea that the monarch is appointed by God and that opposition to him or her is therefore sinful.

Doctrines The rules and teachings of a religious belief.

Gentry The landowning classes below the nobility.

Gospels The first four books of the New Testament of the Bible.

Grace God's favour and forgiveness of sins.

Heretics People who follow teachings that are contrary to rules taught by the Church, either Protestant or Catholic.

Illegitimate Describes a child who was born to unmarried parents.

Inquisition An institution founded by the Catholic Church to discover and punish heretics.

Intolerance Lack of respect for the beliefs of others.

Martyr Someone who suffers death rather than renounce his or her beliefs.

Mass The celebration of Christ's Last Supper, when bread and wine are offered as symbols of Christ's body and blood.

Medieval Relating to the Middle Ages, the period from about AD 1000 to 1500.

Papacy The office of the Pope; the system of government of the Roman Catholic Church.

Penances Punishments to show repentance for sins.

Persecution The ill-treatment of people because of their race or religion.

Popery An insulting term for Roman Catholicism.

Predestination The belief that the salvation of mankind is preordained (decreed) by God.

Presbyterian Relating to the Presbyterian Church, a Protestant Church similar to Calvinism.

Propaganda Ideas spread by governments to serve their own interests.

Puritans Those Protestants who wished to 'purify' the Church of England, removing any remaining traces of Catholicism.

Reformation The religious and political movement of the sixteenth century, which began as an attempt to reform the Catholic Church and ended with the establishment of Protestant Churches.

Sacrament A religious ceremony of the Christian Church such as baptism, marriage, mass (or eucharist).

Salvation In the Christian religion, deliverance from the power of sin.

Theology The study of religion.

Tolerate To respect the beliefs of others.

Books to Read

A Wider World, The Making of the United Kingdom by Rosemary Kelly (Stanley Thorne, 1992)

Spotlight on the English Civil War by Tom Gibb (Wayland, 1987)

The Making of the United Kingdom by Peter Hepplewhite and Neil Tonge (Causeway Press, 1992)

The Making of the United Kingdom by Patricia Kenney (Heinemann, 1996)

The Making of the United Kingdom by Joe Scott (Heinemann, 1993)

For older readers

The Reformation by Owen Chadwick (Penguin, 1990)

Places of Interest to Visit

Canterbury Cathedral
Canterbury
Kent.

The seat of the Archbishop of Canterbury, the Primate (Head of the Church of England). The Cathedral is also the place where St Thomas Becket, Archbishop and Head of the Catholic Church in England, was murdered in 1170 and is the site of a shrine to his memory.

Fountains Abbey
Near Ripon
Yorkshire.

Founded by Cistercian monks in 1132, the abbey was dissolved by Henry VIII and is now the largest monastic ruin in Britain. The abbey ruins belong to the National Trust and can be visited on most days throughout the year.

Hampton Court Palace
East Molesey
Surrey.

The Thameside palace of Cardinal Wolsey. It later became a royal palace when Henry VIII acquired it and added to the building.

The Tolbooth
The Royal Mile
Edinburgh.

The site where John Knox preached many of his sermons.

Westminster Abbey
Westminster
London.

This church, founded by King Edward the Confessor in the tenth century, was built on the site of a Benedictine monastery. It is the place where most English monarchs since William I (1066) have been crowned.

Index

Numbers in **bold** refer to pictures

Act of Supremacy 15, 16, 32
Act of the Six Articles 18
Act of Uniformity 18
Anglican Church (see Church of
    England)
anti-Catholic propaganda **13**
Aske, Robert 17, 18

Calvin, John 26–8, **26**
Calvinism 27
    in England 28
    in Scotland 29–30
Catholic Church 4, 44
    abuses 9
    power of 7, 9
    rites in **5**, 6, **6**
    sense of unity of 8
Catholic plots 25, 32
Charles I 31, 33, **33**, 34–7
    belief in Divine Right 33, **33**
    attitude to Catholics 34
    sets up standard for civil war
        36
    execution 39, 40, **40**
Charles II 41, **41**
Church of England 15, 18, 24, 31,
    33, 34, 43, 44
Commonwealth, the 40
Covenant, the 30, 35
Cranmer, Archbishop Thomas 18,
    18, 23
    Book of Common Prayer 18, 24
    burnt at the stake 23
Cromwell, Oliver **37**, 38, 39, 40

Dissenters 41, 43, 44

Edward VI 18

Elizabeth I 24, 25, **25**
    moderation in religion 24, **25**
    signs death warrant for Mary,
        Queen of Scots 25

English Civil War 37–40
Erasmus 8, **8**, 14

George I **43**
'Glorious Revolution' **42**, 43
Grey, Lady Jane 21
Gunpowder Plot 32, **32**

Hamilton, Patrick 29
Henrician Reformation 15–19
Henry VIII 15, **15**, 16, 32
    appoints himself Head of the
        Church in England 15
    divorces and remarries 16
    dissolves the monasteries 16,
        18

James VI and I 31, **31**
    attitude to Church of England
        31
    produces King James Bible 32
    belief in Divine Right 32
James II 41
    favours Catholics 42
    flees to France 43

Kett, Robert 19
Knox, John 29, **29**, 30, **30**

Laud, Archbishop William 33, **34**
Laudian Church 33, 34–5, 38
Locke, John 43
Luther, Martin 10–14, **10**, **11**
    criticizes concepts of the
        Catholic Church 10
    preaches doctrine of
        Justification by Faith Alone
        10
    nails theses to Church door 11
    summoned to the Emperor's
        court **11**

Mary I 20, **20**
    brings back Catholicism 21–2
    marries Philip II of Spain 22–3

Mary, Queen of Scots 25, 29, **29**,
    30, **30**
Massacre of St Bartholomew's
    Eve 21
Methodist Religion 43, 44
monasteries 6, 7, 9, 16–17
    dissolution of 16, **17**, 18
monks 6, 9, **9**
More, Thomas 16

Newton, Isaac 43, **43**

Pilgrimage of Grace 17
Pope, 7, **7**, 9, 11, 15, **16**
    power of 7, **7**
predestination, belief in 10, 26
Presbyterian Church 29, 30, 38, 39
printing presses 8, 11, **12**, 28
priests, role of **5**, 6, **6**
Protestant Church, establishment
    of **10**
Protestants 4
    persecution of 12, **21**, 23, **23**
Protestant sects 12
Puritans **24**, 25, 26–8, **28**
    persecution of 34

St Augustine 10
Scotland
    Calvinism in 29–30
    hatred of Catholics 29
    Presbyterian Church
        established in 29, 30
Spanish Inquisition 22
    auto-da-fé 22, **22**

Tyndale, William 14, 31
    prints first English Bible 14, **14**

Wesley, John 43, 44, **44**
William III 43
    defeats James II at Battle of
        Boyne 43
Wolsey, Cardinal Thomas 15, **16**
Wycliffe, John 12, **13**